DIALLO K. BROOKS

Bold Quiet Warrior:
Black Men, Leadership, and Justice Work

Part of the Bold Quiet Warrior series

First edition
Civic Vision Press · Washington, DC
boldquietwarrior.com · civicvisionstrategies.com

Contents

Preface
Acknowledgments

PART I — GROUNDING THE CALL
1. Justice Work Requires Black Men's Leadership
2. Freeing Ourselves From What Pulls Us Away From Leadership

PART II — LEADING FROM WHOLENESS
3. Leading From Wholeness
4. Leading for the Long Haul
5. Preparing What Comes

PART III — LEADERSHIP WHEN IT COUNTS
6. Navigating Power, Conflict, and Responsibility
7. The Interior Work
8. Moral Responsibility When Power Is Real

PART IV — STAYING ORIENTED IN THE WORK
9. Why You're Leading
10. Leading in the Moment
11. Holding the North Star
12. Closing: Staying in the Work

About the Author
A Tool for the Work (Appendix)

Preface

This book grows out of a conviction that has shaped my work for more than two decades: justice work needs Black men — not as symbols, not as emergency responders, but as rooted, committed participants in the life of our communities.

The first book in this series explored the inner discipline of leadership — the practices of presence, restraint, and reflection that shape how we show up in the world. This book builds on that foundation, turning more directly toward the collective responsibility of leading in real time, particularly within the work of justice and community building.

The phrase Bold Quiet Warrior comes from my name — Diallo Kamau — and from a lineage rooted in the history of the African Diaspora. It reflects a way of being that holds strength without being driven by ego, quiet without hiding passively, and endurance without being lost in spectacle and fame. It names a leadership tradition that has always existed among our people, even when it has gone unrecognized or been deliberately obscured.

Black men have always stood in roles of leadership — within families, communities, movements, and institutions. This book does not seek to introduce something new, but to align with and continue that call. It centers Black men not to diminish the leadership of Black women or others who have always carried movements forward, but to speak directly to a truth that is often distorted: justice work needs Black men who are grounded, present, and willing to stand in the moment.

This volume is both a call to action and a grounding. It is rooted in history and oriented toward progress, asking us to unlearn what no longer feeds our better selves while modernizing how we understand and practice leadership. It challenges the myths and attacks that seek to divide and devalue Black men, while offering a vision of leadership that creates healthier environments for that leadership to exist organically.

This is not a book about chasing leadership or positioning ourselves at the center of movements. It is about supporting the work, understanding leadership as part of a broader ecosystem, and recognizing that leadership takes many forms — some visible, many not. What follows is an invitation — not to perform leadership, but to practice it. To lead with intention, to stay when the work is slow, and to build something worthy of the people who will inherit it.

Acknowledgments

This book exists because of people — people who have stood in the gap for justice, often without recognition, and who continue to show up every day to shape the world we are living in and the one we are trying to build. I am deeply grateful to the women and men who have taught me, trained me, challenged me, and modeled what it means to lead with integrity, care, and commitment. From faith leaders to community organizers, from seasoned movement builders to young leaders pushing us forward, your work has shaped my understanding of leadership in ways that go deeper than I can fully name.

Change is constant and inevitable. How that change happens depends on the energy we give to shaping it. Much of my motivation comes from people working inside movement spaces, but also from those whose leadership shows up in quieter ways — through consistency, courage, and care. To all who have poured into me, listened to me, and walked alongside me in this work, thank you.

I want to acknowledge my close friends — Antoine, Kamau, Micah, and Rob — my crew and my brothers. Your friendship, honesty, and presence have grounded me more than you know. To my teammates and friends from college, especially Richard (Tech), Ben, Johnnie, Chauncey, Rob, and the entire Shepherd crew, thank you for the lessons learned on and off the court, and for the bonds that continue to shape me. To my coaches at every level, thank you for teaching me that leadership is foundational in sports and in life.

A special acknowledgment is owed to Scott Bradford Doleman, who is no longer with us. Scott was my roommate, teammate, Shepherd University Hall of Famer, and one of the co-founders of United Brothers during our college years. He was a leader on the court and in life, and an even better friend. His influence remains with me, and his example continues to guide how I think about leadership, loyalty, and showing up for others.

I also want to give a particular acknowledgment to Rev. Ernest Lyles Sr., who was one of the most important people in my development during my time at Shepherd. He ran the Multicultural Leadership Program — a space that stretched me, challenged me, and helped me understand what it meant to lead across difference with intention and care. He was also the faculty advisor for United Brothers, the organization I helped found, and his steady presence and guidance shaped what that community became. Rev. Lyles believed in us when we were still figuring ourselves out, and that kind of investment leaves a mark that doesn't go away. I carry what he poured into me, and I'm grateful for every bit of it.

I also want to acknowledge three men who had more to do with who I am than they probably realize. Uncle Buddy — Saint Elmo Crawford Jr., my mother's brother. Uncle Johnny Mickens III, my mother's first cousin, who stepped into that uncle role the way only family can. And Uncle Michael Bonner, my father's first cousin. Each of them came through for me at a different point in my life, at moments when I was still figuring out what it meant to be a man and needed someone who had already walked some of that road. They showed up — sometimes with advice, sometimes just with presence, sometimes simply by being the kind of men worth watching. I carry something from each of them, and I'm grateful this book gives me a place to say it out loud.

Beyond family, there are leaders who shaped this work directly. I am grateful to the movement leaders who opened doors and trusted me early in my career, and to the leaders engaged in this work right now — in the streets, in the courtrooms, in the organizing rooms, and in the institutions where change is contested every day. You have shaped how I understand leadership in ways I can't always trace back to a single moment but feel every time I step into a room. Your courage, care, and consistency remind me why this work matters and why it must be done with integrity and purpose.

I also want to acknowledge my colleagues across the organizations I have had the privilege to work with, as well as the members of the boards I serve on and alongside. Co-creating with you, supporting organizations together, and navigating the responsibilities of leadership has shaped my practice and deepened my understanding of what this work actually requires day to day. Thank you for the trust, the partnership, and the shared commitment to building something that lasts.

To the many young and seasoned elected leaders I have worked with and trained, and to the countless movement leaders and coalition partners I have stood alongside — thank you for your collaboration, your honesty, and your dedication to the work. You remind me that none of this happens alone.

Finally, to my wife, my children, my grandson, my mom, my siblings, and my entire family — thank you for being my reason why. You keep me grounded, honest, and clear about what matters most. This work requires partnership, support systems, and friendship, and I am grateful beyond words for the love and community that make this work possible.

I also want to acknowledge the ancestors whose lives and labor made this work possible. The social justice warriors, civil rights leaders, Black Power movement organizers, and freedom fighters who laid the foundation for collective liberation long before many of us were born. Their courage, discipline, and sacrifice shaped the paths we walk today. We inherit not only their victories, but their unfinished work, and it is because of them that we are able to imagine and build toward freedom with clarity and purpose.

There are many more names that could be written here, and many more stories that deserve to be told. To all who labor for justice, in ways large and small — this book is shaped by you.

PART I

Grounding the Call

This opening section names what has always been true: justice work depends on Black men's leadership, not as symbols or emergency responders, but as rooted participants in the life of our communities. These chapters ground the call to lead in history, relationship, and responsibility, while naming the forces that pull us away from the work.

Justice Work Requires Black Men's Leadership

"Leadership has a harder job to do than just choose sides. It must bring sides together."

— Jesse L. Jackson Sr.

Justice work requires Black men's leadership — not as symbols or figureheads, and not as the ones called in only when the crisis is already burning. It requires Black men who are woven into the fabric of their communities, men who lead not through spectacle but through presence, discipline, and care. It requires men who understand that freedom is a collective project, and that our role in it is not optional or occasional, but essential.

This truth is not new. It is as old as our people's struggle for dignity and as familiar as the lessons passed down at kitchen tables and on front porches. I learned it long before I had the language for it — through the quiet strength of my grandmother, the unyielding expectations of my mother, and the legacy of the men whose names I carry. Leadership was never presented to me as performance. It was responsibility. A way of honoring the people who raised me and the communities that shaped me.

I have spent most of my adult life in justice work — not as an observer, but as a Black man shaped by the same forces, contradictions, and responsibilities as the men I stand beside. My journey has taken me into rooms across this country filled with Black men who are already leading, already carrying, already building. Men who show up not for applause, but because their communities depend on them. Men who are often unseen, often unprotected, and yet still committed to the work of making our people free.

Being in community with Black men from all walks of life has taught me something simple and undeniable: we are not waiting to become leaders — we are leading now. The question is not whether Black men are capable. The question is whether our movements, our institutions, and our communities are willing to invest in the leadership we already carry.

Too often, Black men are treated as symbols of strength while being denied the space to practice it. We are invited into justice work only when the crisis is loud enough to demand our presence — what I call ambulance chasing. We are asked to show up in moments of rupture, but not woven into the daily work of building the infrastructure that prevents those ruptures in the first place. That is not leadership. That is extraction.

Justice work cannot survive on extraction. It requires rootedness, consistency, and care. It requires Black men who are not performing leadership, but practicing it — quietly, steadily, and collectively. It requires men who understand that leadership is not about choosing sides, but about bringing people together, building trust, and creating the conditions where communities can thrive.

Lineage, Name, and Contribution

I didn't find my way into this work by accident. I was shaped by people who understood what it meant to pour into others, to build community, and to hold things together when the world made that difficult. In my family, leadership wasn't a title or a performance. It was a way of moving through the world — steady, intentional, and rooted in care.

My grandmother, Mamie, never lectured about leadership. She lived it. You learned by watching how she carried herself, how she tended to people, how she created order and warmth in the same breath. Her strength wasn't loud, but it was unmistakable. In watching her, I learned that steadiness is its own kind of power.

My mother, Nancy, added her own rhythm to that lesson. She believed in showing up — for your people, for your commitments, for the things that matter. She taught me that your name carries weight, not because of what you achieve, but because of how you treat people and how you honor the ones who shaped you. Leadership, in her telling, wasn't something you chased. It was something you embodied.

Behind them were the ancestors whose stories I grew up hearing — builders, organizers, educators, institution-makers. People who understood that justice isn't a moment; it's a long arc shaped by everyday choices. Their lives made clear that community is something you tend to, something you invest in, something you strengthen for the next generation.

I carry their names, but I also carry their example — not as pressure, but as grounding. They showed me that leadership is less about standing out and more about standing with. Less about being exceptional and more about being present. Less about being in front and more about being connected.

And the truth is, this isn't just my story. Every Black man I've met in this work carries a version of it. Different families, different cities, different circumstances — but the same thread running through it. A sense of being shaped by people who gave what they had. A sense of being part of something larger than yourself. A sense of knowing that your presence matters, even when the world doesn't always say so.

When I talk about Black men's leadership, I'm not talking about a handful of well-known figures. I'm talking about the collective — the brothers who mentor young people after work, who build programs and organizations, who hold families steady, who show up in rooms where decisions get made even when those rooms weren't built with them in mind. Men whose contributions rarely make headlines, but always make a difference.

This is the lineage I come from. This is the lineage I've witnessed across the country. And this is the lineage justice work depends on — not occasionally, not symbolically, but every single day.

Being in Community With Black Men Across the Country

My understanding of Black men's leadership didn't begin in meeting rooms or national gatherings. It started with the brothers I grew up with — the ones I laughed with, learned with, got in trouble with, and figured life out alongside. We didn't call it leadership then. We were simply moving through the world together, shaping one another in ways that felt natural and familiar.

That same thread carried into college. At Shepherd, the friendships I formed became more than social connections; they became a foundation. United Brothers grew out of that foundation. We didn't set out to build an organization that would leave a mark — we set out to create a space where Black men could breathe, connect, and be seen. What emerged was something larger than any of us anticipated: a community that helped brothers feel at home on a campus where we were few in number but rich in presence. We built it by listening to what we needed and trusting one another enough to create it together.

The advisors who stood with us — men who understood the terrain better than we did — shaped that space as well. They didn't hover or dictate. They guided. They modeled. They reminded us that leadership wasn't about being in charge, but about being connected, thoughtful, and willing to build something that would last beyond our time there.

Sports added another layer. Being part of a team taught me how Black men show up for one another under pressure — how we communicate without speaking, how we hold each other accountable without shame, how we learn to trust the man next to us when the game is on the line. My coaches, especially the Black coaches, carried a quiet authority that stayed with me. They didn't just teach plays; they taught presence. They taught preparation. They taught how to carry yourself when eyes are on you and when they aren't.

All of that — friends, teammates, coaches, United Brothers — formed the early shape of my understanding. But it continued to deepen in rooms and circles across the country long after college. I've sat with Black men in community centers, church basements, college auditoriums, and conference rooms where the chairs didn't match but the energy did. I've been in spaces where brothers spoke with a clarity that only comes from lived experience, naming what they've carried, what they've survived, and what they're still trying to build.

What I've seen, over and over, is that leadership is already present. Not the kind that makes headlines, but the kind that keeps families steady, guides young people, and holds communities together. I've met brothers who run youth programs after working a full shift, men who organize neighborhood meetings because no one else will, men who show up for their people even when they're tired or stretched thin.

These aren't exceptions. This is who we are.

And when Black men have space to reflect, to breathe, and to speak honestly about what they're navigating, something powerful happens. The room softens. The laughter deepens. The insight sharpens. You can feel the weight lift just enough for possibility to enter. You can feel the collective wisdom rise to the surface — wisdom that's been there all along, waiting for a place to land.

Being in community with Black men has taught me that leadership isn't something we step into only when the world is watching. It's something we practice every day, often quietly and without recognition. It shows up in how we care for our families, how we mentor younger brothers, how we navigate systems that weren't built with us in mind, and how we hold one another with honesty and care.

It has also taught me that Black men don't need to be convinced of our value. We need spaces that honor it. We need room to grow without being reduced to stereotypes or expectations that don't fit who we are. We need communities that understand the difference between calling someone forward and calling someone out, and movements that see us as partners, not props.

Across the country, I've seen what happens when Black men are given space to lead — not in crisis, not as tokens, but as full participants in shaping the future. The conversations deepen. The strategies sharpen. The work becomes more grounded, more sustainable, and more connected to the people it's meant to serve.

Every time I leave one of those gatherings, I'm reminded of something simple: when Black men have space to lead together, we don't just strengthen ourselves — we strengthen the entire community.

Rejecting Tokenism and Ambulance Chasing

One thing I've learned from all these rooms — from childhood friendships to college brotherhoods to national gatherings — is that Black men's leadership is strongest when it is rooted, consistent, and connected. And yet, too often, the world only looks for us in moments of crisis. We are treated like emergency responders — called in when something breaks, when a headline hits, when a community is hurting and someone needs to stand in front of a microphone.

I've seen it happen more times than I can count. A crisis erupts, and suddenly everyone wants Black men on the front line. They want our presence, our voices, our bodies, our labor. They want us to calm the streets, speak to the cameras, or show up in ways that make the moment look managed. But when the crisis passes, the invitations fade. The support dries up. The space closes. And the same systems that needed us in the moment return to operating without us.

That is not leadership. That is extraction.

Leadership isn't something you call on only when the fire is already burning. It is the work that happens before the crisis — the work that prevents the crisis, the work that builds the kind of community where people feel seen, supported, and connected enough to weather whatever comes.

Black men deserve to be part of that work. Not as tokens. Not as symbols. But as full participants in shaping the future. We deserve to be in the rooms where strategies are formed, not just the rooms where damage control is needed. We deserve to be part of the planning, the visioning, and the building — not just the response.

When Black men are included only in moments of urgency, it sends a message — subtle, but deeply felt. It says our value is tied to crisis. It says our presence is reactive, not foundational. It says we are needed for the moment, but not for the movement.

That is not the story we are living. And it is not the story this book is telling.

Black men have always been part of the infrastructure of justice work. We have been organizers, strategists, thinkers, builders, mentors, and steady hands in moments when the world wasn't watching. We have held families together, guided young people, and shaped communities from the inside out. Our leadership is not occasional. It is ongoing. It is woven into the everyday fabric of our lives.

For justice work to be whole, that leadership must be recognized and supported — not just in crisis, but in the slow, steady work of building something that lasts. That means rejecting tokenism. It means refusing roles that are more about optics than impact. It means stepping away from performance and stepping into the power of being fully present, fully human, and fully engaged.

It also means insisting on being part of the infrastructure — not the afterthought.

Because when Black men are part of the foundation, the work is stronger. The community is stronger. The movement is stronger. And the future becomes something we are shaping together, not something we are reacting to.

An Invitation Forward

What I've seen — in my family, in my friendships, in college, in sports, and in movement spaces across the country — is that Black men are already leading. Not in the ways the world often measures leadership, but in the ways that actually hold communities together. And when that leadership is recognized, supported, and connected to the leadership of Black women, something powerful happens. The work becomes fuller. The community becomes stronger. The future becomes something we are shaping together, not something we are reacting to.

This book is written from that place. It is written with the understanding that Black men do not need to be convinced of our worth or our capacity. We need space. We need connection. We need room to bring our full selves to the work without being reduced to crisis, stereotype, or performance. We need to be part of the infrastructure, not the afterthought.

And we need each other.

Justice work is not something any of us can carry alone. It is a collective effort — built on relationships, shaped by community, and strengthened by the ways we show up for one another.

Justice work requires Black men's leadership. Not occasionally. Not symbolically. But woven into the daily fabric of building communities where people are safe, seen, and free. That leadership grows stronger when it is rooted in where we come from, honest about what we carry, and aligned with the women and men standing beside us. The chapters ahead move deeper into that work — not through pressure or performance, but through clarity, connection, and care.

Freeing Ourselves From What Pulls Us Away From Leadership

There comes a point in every Black man's life when he realizes that the world has been trying to shape him into something smaller than who he actually is. Sometimes it happens early, sometimes much later, but the moment is familiar: a quiet awareness that something is pulling at you, tugging you away from your own voice, your own grounding, your own sense of direction.

For some of us, it shows up as doubt. For others, it's exhaustion. For many, it's the slow weight of expectations that were never ours to carry. And for most of us, it's a mix of things — messages we absorbed without noticing, pressures we learned to navigate without naming, roles we stepped into because they seemed safer than being fully seen.

Leadership doesn't disappear in those moments. It just gets buried.

And if we're honest, a lot of what pulls us away from leadership isn't about ability. It's about survival. It's about navigating systems that weren't built for us, workplaces that don't understand us, communities that rely on us, and histories that live in our bodies whether we acknowledge them or not. It's about trying to move forward while carrying things we never had the chance to set down.

I've seen this in brothers across the country — in their stories, in their posture, in the way they talk about their lives. I've seen it in myself too. The tension between who we are and who the world tells us to be. The pressure to stay composed even when we're stretched thin. The instinct to keep moving even when something inside us is asking for a pause.

This chapter is about that pause.

It's about naming the forces that pull us away from our own leadership — not to dwell on them, but to loosen their grip. It's about giving ourselves permission to look at what we've been carrying and decide what still belongs to us and what doesn't. It's about reclaiming the parts of ourselves that got quiet, not because they were weak, but because they were protecting us.

And it's about understanding that healing isn't separate from leadership. Healing is leadership. It's the work that allows us to show up whole, to show up steady, to show up in ways that strengthen the people around us instead of draining us.

Black men are often expected to lead without tending to ourselves. To carry without resting. To give without receiving. To show strength without showing need. But leadership rooted in depletion doesn't last. Leadership rooted in wholeness does.

This chapter is an invitation to return to ourselves — not the version shaped by pressure or performance, but the version shaped by truth, by community, by the people who poured into us, and by the future we're trying to build.

Because before we can lead others well, we have to be able to hear our own voice again.

Returning to Ourselves

There's a kind of quiet work Black men do that rarely gets named. It's the work of finding our way back to ourselves after years of being shaped by forces that never had our wholeness in mind. It's the work of peeling back the layers — expectations, survival strategies, masks we learned to wear — and remembering the parts of us that were always there, waiting for room to breathe.

Some of this work happens slowly, almost without us noticing. A moment of honesty with a friend. A conversation that hits a little deeper than expected. A memory that resurfaces and asks to be understood differently. Other times, it comes all at once — a realization, a breaking point, a shift that makes it impossible to keep moving the same way.

What I've learned is that returning to ourselves isn't about fixing anything. It's about reconnecting. It's about giving ourselves permission to be human in a world that often treats us like symbols or threats. It's about recognizing that the parts of us that got quiet weren't weak — they were protecting something sacred.

There are patterns I've seen in this work, both in my own life and in the lives of brothers I've walked alongside. We start listening to the voice we've been ignoring — the one that knows when we're tired, when we're stretched thin, when we're carrying too much. We begin questioning the roles we've been performing, not because they were wrong, but because they may no longer fit. The strong one. The fixer. The one who never asks for help. Those roles kept us safe, but they can also keep us small. We allow ourselves to feel what we've been holding — not to drown in it, but to release it. We reconnect with people who see us clearly, who speak to our strength without ignoring our tenderness. And we remember that healing is not a detour from leadership. It is part of it.

This internal work isn't linear. It doesn't follow a neat timeline. Some days we feel centered; other days we feel pulled in every direction. But every time we choose to return to ourselves — to pause, to breathe, to reflect, to reconnect — we strengthen the foundation our leadership rests on.

And the truth is, Black men have always done this work. Quietly. Steadily. In ways that don't always get acknowledged. We've learned how to navigate a world that misreads us, how to protect our joy, how to build community even when the odds are stacked against us. We've learned how to carry our stories with dignity, even when the world tries to rewrite them.

Returning to ourselves is not about becoming someone new. It's about remembering who we've always been.

We Don't Return to Ourselves Alone

One of the most important things I've learned — and had to relearn — is that returning to ourselves is not something Black men do in isolation. It's not a solo journey. It's not a test of endurance. And it's not something we grind or hustle our way through.

The world often tells us otherwise. It tells us that strength means handling everything on our own. That healing is private. That if we just push harder, work longer, stay busy enough, we'll eventually find our way back to ourselves. But the grind doesn't bring us home. Hustling might help us survive a season, but it doesn't help us heal.

Healing happens in relationship. It happens in community. It happens with support. It happens when we allow ourselves to be held, challenged, and guided by people who understand the terrain we're navigating.

Black men have never healed alone. We've always done this work together — in conversation, in shared silence, in spaces where we could finally exhale. What's different now is that we're naming it with intention. We're recognizing that returning to ourselves requires structure, care, and support, not just willpower.

For many of us, that means therapy — a space where we can speak freely, unpack what we've been carrying, and learn new ways of understanding ourselves. It means mentors and elders who have done their own healing work and can offer perspective without judgment. It means brothers who are willing to be honest about their own journeys, not as examples of perfection, but as proof that growth is possible.

It also means building support structures that don't disappear when things get hard. Communities that don't just celebrate our strength, but make room for our vulnerability. Relationships that don't demand performance, but invite presence. Spaces where we can learn from people who are further along the path — not because they have all the answers, but because they've learned how to listen to themselves more clearly.

This kind of return doesn't happen by accident. It has to be intentional. It requires us to choose connection over isolation, support over silence, healing over hustle. It requires us to believe that we deserve care, not just because we're struggling, but because we're human.

And when Black men return to ourselves this way — supported, grounded, connected — our leadership changes. We lead with more clarity. More patience. More depth. We stop reacting and start responding. We stop performing strength and start practicing wholeness.

Returning to ourselves is not about doing more. It's about being held well enough to become more of who we already are.

A Charge Forward

Returning to ourselves is not the end of the work. It's the beginning of how we lead differently.

When Black men choose healing over hustle, connection over isolation, and support over silence, we don't just change our own lives — we change the way leadership shows up in our families, our communities, and our movements. We lead with more clarity. More patience. More courage. We stop reacting to the world's expectations and start responding from a place that is grounded and whole.

This is the charge: be intentional about your return. Be deliberate about the spaces you enter, the people you learn from, and the support you allow yourself to receive. Seek out community that strengthens you. Invest in healing that helps you hear your own voice again. Learn from people who have done the work and are willing to walk alongside you — not as saviors, but as companions on the path.

Leadership rooted in wholeness is not passive. It is disciplined, deliberate, and powerful in ways that don't always announce themselves but always leave a mark. The work ahead asks Black men to lead from that place — not hardened, not depleted, not alone, but connected, supported, and clear about who we are and what we're building.

Return to yourself — and then lead from there.

Leading From Wholeness

Leadership that lasts is shaped long before it is truly tested. This section focuses on the inner work that sustains Black men in justice work over time, exploring the practices and commitments that make leadership possible without burning us out or pulling us apart.

Leading From Wholeness

Leadership changes when it's no longer driven by survival.

When Black men return to ourselves — supported, grounded, and clear — we don't just feel different. We lead differently. The urgency softens. The posture shifts. The need to prove gives way to the ability to listen. What emerges is a kind of leadership that is steady, relational, and deeply rooted in purpose.

This chapter is about that shift.

For many of us, leadership has been shaped by pressure. Pressure to perform. Pressure to represent. Pressure to carry more than our share. We learned to lead while bracing ourselves — anticipating resistance, guarding our emotions, staying alert to how we might be perceived. That kind of leadership can be effective in moments, but it's exhausting over time.

Leadership rooted in wholeness feels different.

It doesn't rush to fill silence. It doesn't confuse volume with authority. It doesn't rely on constant motion to feel legitimate. Instead, it's grounded. It's thoughtful. It's responsive rather than reactive. It's shaped by a deep understanding of self and a clear sense of responsibility to others.

I've seen this kind of leadership in Black men who have taken the time to heal — to reflect, to reconnect, to build community around themselves. They don't lead from ego or fear. They lead from clarity. They know who they are, what they value, and what they're willing to stand for. And because of that, people trust them.

Leading from wholeness doesn't mean we stop being challenged. It means we stop being destabilized by every challenge. We can hold complexity without losing ourselves. We can navigate conflict without becoming hardened. We can show strength without abandoning tenderness.

This kind of leadership shows up in small, consistent ways. It listens before responding, especially when the stakes are high. It sets boundaries that protect energy and integrity. It invites others into leadership rather than carrying everything alone. It stays connected to community even when the work gets demanding — and it returns to itself regularly, not just when something breaks. These aren't abstract ideals. They're choices made every day about how we show up, how we engage, and how we care for ourselves and others.

Leading from wholeness also means understanding that our leadership is not just about outcomes — it's about impact. It's about the culture we create, the relationships we nurture, and the example we set for those watching us, especially younger Black men who are still figuring out what leadership can look like.

When Black men lead from wholeness, we give others permission to do the same. We model a way of being that says strength and care are not opposites. That healing and leadership are not separate paths. That justice work can be both disciplined and humane.

This chapter is an invitation to step into that kind of leadership — not perfectly, not all at once, but intentionally. To lead from a place that is grounded in who you are, supported by community, and guided by a vision larger than yourself.

What Changes When We Lead From Wholeness

I've seen the difference wholeness makes in real time.

I've been in rooms where Black men were leading from a place of depletion — tired, guarded, carrying more than they could name. The work still moved forward, but it moved with tension. Conversations stayed surface-level. Decisions felt rushed. People spoke, but they weren't always heard. Leadership in those moments was about holding things together, not building something new.

And I've been in rooms where Black men were leading from wholeness.

The difference is immediate. The pace slows just enough for clarity to enter. People listen more than they speak. There's less posturing, less urgency to prove something. The work feels steadier, not because the challenges are smaller, but because the leaders are grounded in who they are.

Leading from wholeness doesn't mean the work gets easier. It means we stop making it harder than it needs to be.

I've watched brothers lead meetings without dominating them. I've seen men pause a conversation not to control it, but to make sure everyone was actually present. I've seen leaders name uncertainty without losing authority, and set boundaries without apology. Those moments don't always look dramatic, but they change the culture of a space.

Wholeness-based leadership refuses a few things quietly, without announcement. It refuses the idea that leadership has to be loud to be effective. It refuses the pressure to perform strength instead of practicing clarity. It refuses the belief that urgency is the same as importance.

Instead, it makes room for thoughtfulness. It makes room for relationship. It makes room for people to bring their full selves into the work.

I've seen this most clearly in moments of tension — when decisions had to be made, when conflict surfaced, when the stakes were high. Leaders grounded in wholeness don't rush to control the moment. They stay present. They ask better questions. They trust the process enough to let it unfold without forcing it.

That kind of leadership builds trust. Not because it promises certainty, but because it models integrity.

And it's contagious.

When Black men lead from wholeness, others begin to show up differently too. The room becomes more honest. The work becomes more collaborative. People stop bracing themselves and start engaging more fully. The leadership doesn't sit at the top of the room — it moves through it.

This is what happens when healing is not treated as separate from leadership, but as its foundation.

Reclaiming Masculinity Without Losing Ourselves

Part of leading from wholeness means being honest about the traits many of us were taught to carry as men — and being willing to ask whether they still serve us or the communities we're responsible for.

For a long time, masculinity was presented to many of us as something narrow and rigid. Don't show emotion. Don't ask for help. Don't slow down. Don't soften. Strength was measured by how much we could endure without breaking, how little we revealed, how tightly we stayed in control. Those lessons didn't come from nowhere. They were shaped by history, by survival, by the need to navigate a world that often treated Black men as threats before it treated us as human.

But just because those traits were learned doesn't mean they are permanent. And just because they helped us survive doesn't mean they help us lead.

I'm careful not to call masculinity itself toxic. Being masculine is not the problem. The problem is when the version of masculinity we inherit cuts us off from our full humanity — when it teaches us to suppress instead of process, dominate instead of connect, endure instead of heal. When that happens, the effects don't stop with us. They show up in our leadership, our relationships, and the communities we serve.

Jason Wilson, author of Battle Cry and founder of the Cave of Adullam Transformational Training Academy, names this dynamic as emotional incarceration — the way men are taught to confine parts of themselves in the name of strength, only to find that confinement shaping how they show up everywhere else.

I've seen the effects of this kind of conditioning in leadership spaces. Men who feel they have to have all the answers. Men who struggle to listen because listening feels like weakness. Men who confuse control with responsibility. None of this comes from bad intent. It comes from being taught a version of manhood that leaves little room for reflection, vulnerability, or growth.

Leading from wholeness asks something different of us. It asks us to recognize that some of the traits we picked up along the way — hyper-control, emotional distance, constant toughness — may have helped us survive, but they can have harmful effects if we never question them. They can limit trust. They can shut down collaboration. They can make leadership feel heavy instead of shared.

Wholeness doesn't require us to abandon masculinity. It asks us to expand it. To understand that strength includes emotional awareness. That courage includes honesty. That leadership includes the ability to be changed by the people we're responsible to.

When Black men allow ourselves to redefine masculinity in this way, we don't lose authority — we gain depth. We don't become less effective — we become more trustworthy. We don't weaken our leadership — we humanize it.

And that kind of leadership doesn't just feel better. It builds healthier communities, stronger movements, and more sustainable paths forward.

Wholeness in Relationship and Responsibility

Leading from wholeness doesn't stop with personal clarity. It shows up most clearly in how we relate to others — especially in spaces where power, history, and responsibility intersect.

For Black men, leadership has never existed in isolation. It has always been shaped in relationship — with Black women, with other men, with elders, with young people, with community. When we lead from a place of wholeness, those relationships change. Not because the work becomes easier, but because it becomes more honest.

I've seen how leadership shifts when Black men stop leading from posture and start leading from presence. Conversations become less about control and more about collaboration. Listening becomes an act of strength, not concession. Accountability becomes something we practice together, not something we avoid or deflect.

This matters deeply in our relationships with Black women. Wholeness-based leadership refuses the idea that leadership is something Black men do over or ahead of others. It recognizes that Black women have always been leaders — often carrying the work when men were absent, silenced, or pushed aside. Leading from wholeness means showing up in partnership, not competition. It means respecting wisdom that doesn't look like our own. It means being willing to be challenged without becoming defensive.

That kind of leadership doesn't diminish us. It strengthens the work.

The same is true in our relationships with other men. When Black men lead from wholeness, we create space for other men to do the same. We stop reinforcing narrow definitions of strength. We stop rewarding silence and emotional distance. We model a way of being that says leadership includes care, reflection, and responsibility to one another.

This kind of leadership also changes how we hold power. Leaders grounded in wholeness don't cling to authority. They share it. They understand that leadership is not about being indispensable, but about building capacity in others. They invest in people, not just outcomes. They think beyond the moment and toward sustainability.

Responsibility, in this sense, is not about carrying everything alone. It's about stewarding relationships well. It's about knowing when to step forward and when to step back. It's about creating conditions where others can lead, grow, and contribute fully.

When Black men lead this way, leadership stops being something people endure and becomes something people trust. Not because it's perfect or effortless — but because it's grounded, relational, and accountable to the people it serves. That kind of leadership doesn't just change outcomes. It changes culture.

Leading for the Long Haul

"Don't ask what the world needs. Ask what makes you come alive, and go do it. Because what the world needs is people who have come alive."

— Howard Thurman

Leadership doesn't end when clarity arrives. In many ways, that's when the real work begins.

Clarity gives us direction, but it doesn't carry us forward on its own. What follows is practice — the steady, often unremarkable work of showing up with intention, even when the path isn't obvious and the progress isn't immediate. This is where leadership becomes less about momentum and more about commitment.

For Black men, this part of the journey is often the hardest. We are used to responding to urgency. We know how to mobilize in moments of crisis. We know how to push through when the stakes are high and the pressure is on. But leadership for the long haul asks something different of us. It asks us to stay present when the work slows down. To remain grounded when recognition fades. To keep showing up when there is no clear finish line in sight.

This kind of leadership requires discipline — not the kind rooted in self-denial or constant sacrifice, but the kind rooted in care. It means developing rhythms that allow us to sustain ourselves and the work at the same time. It means understanding that burnout is not a badge of honor, and exhaustion is not proof of commitment.

Leading for the long haul also means resisting the pull of urgency culture. Not every moment requires immediate action. Not every challenge demands a reaction. Sometimes leadership looks like waiting, listening, and allowing space for others to step forward. Sometimes it looks like saying no — not because the work isn't important, but because doing everything is not the same as doing what matters most.

I've seen how leadership changes when Black men give themselves permission to slow down without disengaging. Decisions become more thoughtful. Relationships deepen. The work becomes more sustainable. Leaders stop measuring their impact by how busy they are and start measuring it by how well the work holds over time.

This kind of leadership also asks us to let go of the idea that we have to be indispensable. Leading for the long haul means building collective strength, not personal centrality. It means trusting others with responsibility. It means creating systems and cultures that don't collapse when one person steps away.

There is a quiet confidence that comes with this approach. A steadiness that doesn't need constant affirmation. A sense of purpose that isn't shaken by setbacks or delays. This is leadership that understands its role in something larger — something that will outlast any single moment, campaign, or individual.

Leading for the long haul is not about doing more. It's about doing what is necessary, consistently, with care.

And when Black men lead this way, we create space for leadership that endures — leadership that remains grounded, humane, and accountable, even when the work is slow and the road is long.

Building What Lasts

Howard Thurman understood that leadership rooted only in urgency eventually collapses under its own weight. His insistence on inner life was not a retreat from justice work, but a strategy for sustaining it. He believed that movements endure when they are grounded in purpose, not just reaction.

That grounding matters when we begin to think beyond moments and toward institutions.

Leading for the long haul means shifting our imagination. It means asking not only what needs to change now, but what needs to be built so that change can hold. Institutions — whether formal organizations, community networks, or cultural practices — are how values become durable. They are how leadership outlives individuals.

This is where the ethic of the Bold Quiet Warrior becomes most clear.

To be bold is to imagine a more just world without apology. To name what is possible even when the evidence feels thin. To believe that equity, dignity, and care are not abstract ideals, but achievable commitments.

To be quiet is to practice listening and learning. To resist the need to dominate every space. To understand that wisdom often emerges slowly, through relationship, reflection, and shared effort.

And to be a warrior is not to seek conflict, but to bring discipline to the work. To stay committed when progress is uneven. To develop the patience, strategy, and resilience required for social and racial justice over time.

African wisdom reminds us that speed is not the same as progress. If you want to go fast, go alone. If you want to go far, go together. Institutions are how we go far. They require collaboration, trust, and a willingness to share leadership. They demand that we think beyond ourselves and invest in structures that can carry the work forward.

This kind of leadership understands that a rising tide truly does lift all ships — not through shortcuts or spectacle, but through sustained, collective effort. When Black men lead with this long view, we help create conditions where everyone benefits. Where justice work is not a sprint, but a shared journey.

Leading for the long haul is not about doing more. It's about stewardship. It's about building something worthy of the people who will inherit it.

And that is the work of the Bold Quiet Warrior.

Each One, Teach One

Institutions do not sustain themselves. People do.

One of the most enduring ways leadership carries forward is through mentorship that is rooted in relationship rather than hierarchy. At its best, mentorship is not about instruction alone, but about shared practice and mutual responsibility. The tradition of each one, teach one has always reflected this understanding, emphasizing the passing down of care, reflection, and accountability alongside knowledge.

This kind of mentorship is not about reproducing ourselves or preserving a single model of leadership. It is about preparing others to lead in their own voice, with clarity and grounding, while remaining connected across generations. Leadership, in this sense, is not something we hand off and walk away from, but something we practice together over time.

For me, mentorship has never been a one-way exchange. It's a space of mutual learning. While younger people may come seeking guidance, they also bring clarity — often in the form of unfiltered honesty about the world they're navigating. Their questions are sharper. Their reactions are less rehearsed. Their critiques are shaped by conditions that are constantly changing. Listening to young people has kept me grounded as I've grown older. It has reminded me that leadership is not static.

Healthy leaders understand this. They don't approach mentorship as a way to reproduce themselves. They approach it as a way to prepare others to lead in their own voice. They guide without forcing. They offer context without control. They create space for growth rather than demanding replication.

This is where the discipline of the Bold Quiet Warrior shows up again.

Bold enough to believe deeply in the potential of the next generation — even when their approach challenges our own.

Quiet enough to listen more than we speak, and allow room for experimentation, failure, and learning.

Disciplined enough to show up consistently, modeling integrity, patience, and accountability over time.

I've learned as much from those I've mentored as they may have learned from me. Their honesty has sharpened my thinking. Their urgency has challenged my assumptions. Their creativity has expanded my imagination. In that exchange, leadership becomes shared — not diluted, but strengthened.

This is how institutions remain alive. Not through rigid preservation, but through thoughtful transmission. When Black men lead with this understanding, we help ensure that the work doesn't end with us. We prepare others not just to inherit leadership, but to reshape it.

Each one, teach one is not a slogan, but a practice.

Preparing What Comes

Leadership that lasts is never accidental. It is shaped by what we choose to pass on, and by how intentionally we prepare others to lead without us.

By the time we reach this point in the work, the question is no longer whether leadership matters. The question is whether it will endure. That endurance depends less on individual strength and more on collective readiness. It depends on whether we have invested in people, practices, and institutions that can carry the work forward when we step back.

For Black men, this moment asks us to think differently about legacy. Not as recognition or reputation, but as preparation. Legacy is not what people say about us when we are gone. It is who is ready because we were here.

Preparing what comes next requires humility. It requires us to accept that the future will not look exactly like the past, and that leadership must evolve to meet new realities. Young people are not simply inheritors of our work; they are interpreters of it. They see the world with fresh eyes, shaped by conditions we did not face in the same way. Their honesty can be uncomfortable, but it is also clarifying.

Healthy leaders understand that preparation is not about control. It is about guidance. It is about creating space for others to grow into leadership without forcing them into our image. This means modeling values rather than prescribing outcomes. It means sharing context, not commands. It means trusting that the next generation will carry the work forward in ways that reflect both continuity and change.

Institutions play a critical role here. When leadership is tied too closely to personality, it becomes fragile. When it is rooted in shared values and collective practice, it becomes resilient. Institutions that last are those that make room for learning, adaptation, and renewal. They are shaped by listening as much as by vision.

This is where the ethic of the Bold Quiet Warrior continues to guide the work. To be bold is to imagine a future that is more just than the present, and to commit to building toward it even when the path is uncertain. To be quiet is to listen deeply, especially to those whose experiences challenge our assumptions. And to be a warrior is to bring discipline to the process, understanding that justice work requires patience, strategy, and sustained effort.

Preparing what comes next is not about stepping aside prematurely, nor is it about holding on too tightly. It is about knowing when to lead, when to support, and when to make room. It is about ensuring that leadership is not a bottleneck, but a bridge.

When Black men lead with this understanding, we help create conditions where leadership is shared, institutions are strengthened, and the work continues with integrity. We prepare others not just to inherit responsibility, but to reshape it in service of a more equitable world.

This is how leadership becomes generational. This is how the work moves forward.

Filling the Gaps We Inherited

I came to this understanding through my own work in education and education justice. Over the past several years, including time spent at the U.S. Department of Education, I saw up close how systems shape opportunity — and how often they fail to reflect the people they are meant to serve.

For Black boys in particular, the absence of Black men in educational spaces is not incidental. Many Black boys move through their entire academic careers without ever having a Black male teacher. They rarely see themselves reflected in positions of authority, care, or intellectual leadership within the classroom. That absence sends a quiet message about who belongs, who leads, and who is expected to succeed.

When representation is missing, mentorship becomes even more critical. If schools and institutions are not consistently providing Black boys with role models who reflect their lived experience, then the responsibility does not disappear. It shifts. It lands on those of us who understand the gap and are willing to step into it with intention.

The same dynamic shows up in professional environments. Black men are often isolated in workplaces where there are few colleagues or supervisors who share their background or understand the terrain they are navigating. I know this experience personally. I've spent much of my career in spaces where I was one of the only Black men in the room, learning to lead without many visible examples to follow.

That isolation is not just personal. It is structural. And it reinforces why mentorship cannot be optional.

This is why I've always been intentional about connecting with younger Black men and women in professional spaces. Not to position myself as an expert, but to offer presence, context, and support. To help them navigate environments that were not designed with them in mind. And just as importantly, to learn from them as they make sense of a world that is changing faster than any one generation can fully grasp.

Mentorship, at its best, is reciprocal. It is not about transferring fixed knowledge from one person to another. It is about staying in conversation. Young people bring a clarity that can be bracing. Their reactions to injustice are often unfiltered. Their questions cut through language that has grown too comfortable. Listening to them keeps leadership honest.

Our role is not to force them into our frameworks. It is to guide them as they develop their own. To offer perspective without imposing certainty. To model growth rather than perfection.

This is how leadership becomes generational. Not through control, but through trust. Not through replication, but through preparation. When Black men step into mentorship with this understanding, we help fill gaps that institutions have left open. We create pathways where none existed. And we ensure that leadership is not something young people have to imagine alone.

What Institutions Must Unlearn

If we are serious about preparing the next generation of leaders, we also have to be honest about what needs to be unlearned.

Many institutions were not designed to cultivate new leadership. They were built to protect stability, preserve hierarchy, and minimize risk. Over time, those instincts harden into gatekeeping practices that limit access, slow growth, and concentrate opportunity in the hands of a few. These patterns do not always come from malice. More often, they are rooted in fear — fear of disruption, fear of losing control, and fear of change.

Leadership that lasts cannot be built on fear.

For institutions to make room for new leadership, they must unlearn the idea that knowledge alone is enough. Information without access does not create opportunity, and advice without advocacy does not open doors. This is where mentorship must evolve into something more intentional and more accountable. This is where sponsorship becomes essential.

Sponsorship goes beyond guidance by using position and influence to create pathways for others. It involves vouching for people when they are not in the room, recommending them for opportunities, introducing them to networks, and helping them navigate systems that were not built with them in mind. Sponsorship is not about favoritism; it is about equity.

When we sponsor others, we are not only sharing what we know. We are sharing what we have access to.

This kind of leadership requires institutions to unlearn gatekeeping as a default posture. Too often, organizations treat access as something to be earned only after long periods of proximity or conformity. That approach slows innovation and reinforces exclusion. Healthy institutions understand that growth depends on circulation, and that new ideas, new leaders, and new perspectives must be allowed to move through the system.

Unlearning gatekeeping also requires rethinking how risk is distributed. Institutions often protect themselves by limiting who is given opportunities to lead. When leadership is concentrated in this way, burnout increases and resilience decreases. Sharing responsibility is not a threat to stability; it is a condition for sustainability.

For Black men working within these systems, this unlearning carries particular weight. Many of us have navigated institutions where access was unclear and advancement felt opaque. We know what it means to be capable but unseen. That experience carries responsibility and calls us to lead differently.

Sponsorship is one way we interrupt the patterns we inherited. It allows us to move from individual success to collective progress and ensures that leadership does not remain locked behind informal rules and unspoken expectations.

Institutions that endure are those willing to make this shift. They understand that leadership is not diminished when it is shared, but strengthened. When mentorship is paired with sponsorship, preparation becomes real. Access expands, growth accelerates, and leadership begins to reflect the full range of talent and possibility within the communities institutions are meant to serve.

When Sponsorship Creates Space to Grow

I learned the power of sponsorship firsthand when I stepped into a director-level role for the first time in my social justice career. It wasn't something I asked for or something I lobbied for. It was something someone else saw in me and chose to act on.

At the time, my supervisor was a Black man who understood both the work and the system we were operating within. As he prepared to leave the organization, he made it clear to senior leadership that I should be promoted into a director role. He didn't do this quietly or hedge — he named it as a strong recommendation for the organization's future.

What mattered most to me was why he used his voice and position to uplift me. He told me that he had watched how I showed up. That I took on the work without complaint, whether it was mundane or high-profile. That I didn't chase visibility, but I didn't shy away from responsibility either. He saw consistency. He saw capacity. And he believed I was ready to grow.

That endorsement changed the trajectory of my career. Without it, I might not have had the opportunity to step into leadership at that moment. And without that growth, I might have decided to leave the work altogether. Social justice work is difficult to sustain when you feel stagnant, when your contributions are invisible, and when there is no clear pathway forward.

What he offered me was not advancement before I was ready. It was opportunity when it was time.

I was told something then that has stayed with me: as you grow, most roles are not positions you already know everything about. They are roles you grow into. You learn by doing. You develop capacity once you are trusted with responsibility. That growth cannot happen if the opportunity never comes.

His sponsorship made that growth possible. He mentored me by modeling leadership. He guided me through the work. And when it mattered most, he used his voice and his position to open a door I could not have opened on my own. That is what ethical sponsorship looks like.

This kind of leadership requires discernment. It requires knowing when someone is ready to stretch, not because they are perfect, but because they have demonstrated the ability to learn, adapt, and lead with integrity. It also requires courage. Sponsorship carries risk. It asks leaders to stand behind their people and trust their judgment.

But the alternative is far more costly. When institutions fail to create pathways for growth, they lose talent. They lose momentum. And they lose people who might otherwise stay committed to the work.

This is how institutions renew themselves. This is how leadership becomes shared rather than hoarded. And this is how the work continues with strength and purpose.

Accountability in Sponsorship

Sponsorship carries responsibility.

When we open doors for others, we are not just creating opportunity. We are shaping the future of leadership within our institutions. That means sponsorship cannot be casual, transactional, or unexamined. It must be practiced with accountability, clarity, and care.

For Black men in leadership, this accountability matters deeply. Too often, we have navigated systems where advancement felt arbitrary, where access depended on proximity rather than preparation, and where expectations were unclear. We know what it feels like to be capable but overlooked. That experience should sharpen our leadership, not harden it.

Accountable sponsorship begins with discernment. It asks us to be honest about readiness without demanding perfection. It requires us to recognize capacity, consistency, and the ability to learn. Sponsorship is not about placing people into roles they are unprepared for. It is about trusting them with opportunity when it is time, and committing to support their growth once they are there.

It also requires follow-through. When we sponsor someone, we are not simply endorsing them and stepping away. We remain invested. We check in. We offer guidance when challenges arise. We help them navigate the unspoken rules of institutions that were not designed with them in mind. Accountability means standing with people beyond the moment of promotion.

Formalizing sponsorship within institutions is one way to ensure this accountability does not depend on chance. Formal sponsorship does not mean rigid programs or prescribed pairings. It means clarity. It means naming sponsorship as a leadership responsibility. It means creating expectations that leaders will actively develop others, open doors, and share access. And it means evaluating leadership not only by outcomes, but by who is being prepared to lead next.

For Black men, this work is both personal and collective. We understand the cost of stagnation. We know how isolating leadership can be when there are few examples to follow. That knowledge carries obligation. It calls us to lead in ways that expand possibility rather than restrict it.

Accountable sponsorship is one way we honor that obligation. This is not about lowering standards. It is about widening access. And when Black men lead with this level of accountability, we help build institutions that are not only effective, but just.

Stepping Up and Stepping Back

Leadership is not a fixed position. It is a practice that requires constant discernment. Knowing when to step up, and knowing when to step back, are equally important skills. Both demand courage. Both demand humility.

For Black men engaged in social and racial justice work, this balance is especially critical. We are often called to lead in moments of crisis, to carry weight when systems fail, and to show up when others retreat. Stepping up is familiar terrain.

Stepping back is harder.

Stepping back does not mean disengaging. It does not mean abandoning responsibility or withdrawing from the work. It means creating space for others to lead, even when we are capable of continuing ourselves. It means trusting the preparation we have invested in others. It means understanding that leadership is not diminished when it is shared.

Bold enough to step forward when leadership is needed, to name injustice clearly, and to imagine a better world without apology.

Quiet enough to listen when others are ready to lead, recognizing that wisdom does not belong to one generation or one voice.

Disciplined enough to step up without ego, and step back without resentment — remaining committed to the mission rather than attached to position.

In social and racial justice movements, this balance determines whether leadership becomes sustainable or stagnant. Movements falter when leadership calcifies, when the same voices dominate, and when new leaders are not trusted with real responsibility. They endure when leadership circulates, when preparation meets opportunity, and when institutions are willing to evolve.

For Black men, stepping back is not about disappearing. It is about stewardship. It is about ensuring that the work continues with strength, integrity, and relevance.

This is the work of the Bold Quiet Warrior. Not to lead forever, but to lead well enough that the work does not end with us.

For Those Waiting to Step Up

There are Black men reading this who are waiting.

Waiting to be asked. Waiting to be invited. Waiting for someone to say, now it's your turn.

That waiting is understandable. Many of us were taught, implicitly or explicitly, that leadership is something granted rather than claimed. We learned to watch closely, to prove ourselves quietly, to wait for recognition in systems that rarely offer it freely. In justice work and in adjacent spaces, that hesitation can feel like caution. Sometimes it is. Other times, it becomes a barrier.

Stepping up does not require permission. It requires readiness and responsibility.

Readiness does not mean knowing everything. It means being willing to learn in public and in private. It means showing up consistently, taking on the work that needs to be done, and developing the discipline to grow inside the role once the opportunity comes. Leadership is rarely something we master before we enter it. We grow into it by doing the work.

For Black men, stepping up is often an act of courage. It means trusting ourselves in spaces that were not built with us in mind. It means believing that our presence, perspective, and leadership matter, even when the system has not affirmed that truth.

But stepping up is only part of the journey. Those who step forward must also prepare themselves for the moment when they will need to step back. Not because they are no longer capable, but because the work demands continuity. Stepping back does not mean disappearing. It means shifting roles. It means moving from being the primary voice to being a steady presence. From leading at the front to supporting from the side. From building momentum to protecting what has been built.

This transition is critical for the health of movements and institutions. When leaders refuse to step back, growth stalls. When leaders step back with intention, leadership multiplies.

Bold enough to step forward when leadership is needed.

Quiet enough to listen when others are ready to lead.

Disciplined enough to know that the work is bigger than any one role or moment.

If you are waiting to step up, know this: your leadership is needed. The world does not require your perfection. It requires your presence, your preparation, and your willingness to grow inside the responsibility once it arrives. And when the time comes to step back, know that your impact does not end — it evolves, deepens, and becomes part of something larger. That is how leadership becomes generational. That is how movements endure. And that is how Black men lead with purpose, humility, and strength in the work of justice.

PART III

Leadership When It Counts

Power changes the landscape of leadership. This section turns toward the moments when leadership is tested by conflict, responsibility, and consequence, examining how Black men navigate those moments with clarity and care while holding moral responsibility when the stakes are high.

Navigating Power, Conflict, and Responsibility

Movements are not immune to power. Even those rooted in justice can become shaped by competition, positioning, and the struggle for platform. I've seen this firsthand. When visibility becomes currency, leadership can drift away from the people and toward performance. The work risks becoming about who is seen rather than who is served.

Bob Moses understood this tension deeply.

For those who may not know him, Bob Moses was a central figure in the Civil Rights Movement and a key leader within the Student Nonviolent Coordinating Committee. He played a pivotal role in Freedom Summer and spent much of his life organizing quietly, deliberately, and with deep respect for the people closest to the work. He was never drawn to the spotlight, though history often placed him there. His leadership was rooted in listening, discipline, and trust in ordinary people to shape extraordinary change.

He once said, "Don't think necessarily of starting a movement. Do what you think actually needs to be done, set an example, and hope your actions will click with someone else."

I had the opportunity to meet Bob Moses many years ago while participating in the first Union Summer program organized by the AFL-CIO. The program was designed to help young leaders connect to the labor movement, and my cohort focused on organizing in the South, retracing the path of Freedom Summer. For me, meeting Bob Moses felt like encountering history — someone I had admired from a distance, someone I knew largely through documentaries like Eyes on the Prize.

What struck me most was not what he said about the past, but what he asked about the future.

Instead of recounting war stories from the Civil Rights Movement, he turned the conversation toward us. He asked a room full of young people, across race and background, how we thought the problems facing the world should be solved. He listened carefully. He challenged gently. He treated our ideas as worthy of consideration.

That moment stayed with me.

Bob Moses was more than the figure I had seen on screen. He was present, curious, and grounded. His leadership was quiet, but never passive. He modeled a way of holding influence without centering himself, of engaging conflict without dominating it, and of keeping the work focused on people rather than a singular personality.

For Black men in social and racial justice movements, this example matters. We are often navigating spaces where power is uneven, where leadership is contested, and where visibility can become mistaken for impact. Competition for platform can pull us away from the work itself. And when that happens, movements lose clarity.

Conflict is not a sign that leadership has failed. It is often a sign that leadership is required. The question is how we navigate it.

This chapter turns outward to examine that reality. It looks at how Black men engage power without becoming hardened by it, how we move through conflict without losing sight of the people, and how responsibility demands discipline, humility, and restraint. Because leadership that lasts is not built on spotlight. It is built on example.

Learning From the Whole Story

Leadership is hard work. Conflict is inevitable when so much is at stake.

Those who came before us navigated conditions that can feel unimaginable today — open violence, state repression, internal division, and constant threat. That reality produced extraordinary courage and sacrifice. It also produced moments of fracture, harm, and limitation.

If we are serious about leadership, we have to be willing to hold all of it.

For Black men in movements for justice, this means resisting the urge to either romanticize the past or dismiss it entirely. Our responsibility is not to judge previous generations from a distance, but to learn from them with honesty — to carry forward what strengthened the work and to refuse to repeat what weakened it.

I often tell younger colleagues and movement leaders that leadership development requires this kind of honesty. We cannot inherit only the parts of leadership that feel inspiring. We also have to study the moments that fell short — the ways power was mishandled, voices were silenced, or people were harmed in the name of progress.

That learning is not about blame. It is about evolution.

Our task is to strengthen our leadership practices so they meet the moment we are in now. That means building in ways that are inclusive, supportive, and grounded in care for people. Movements do not exist without people. Institutions do not survive without trust. If people are not being taken care of, we have to ask ourselves why we are doing this work in the first place.

This is not a call for perfection. It is a call for growth. We all fall short at times. What matters is intentionality and self-accountability — the willingness to reflect, to repair, and to realign with the values we claim to hold.

The north star we march toward is justice — but not justice for its own sake. Justice as collective liberation. Justice as freedom that expands rather than constricts. Justice that leads to healthy, safe, and thriving communities rooted in love and respect.

Conflict does not have to pull us away from that north star. When managed well, conflict can sharpen our focus. It can surface what needs attention. It can create growth rather than division. But that requires discipline. It requires leaders who are willing to stay grounded, to listen deeply, and to keep people at the center of the work.

Bold enough to confront conflict without avoiding it.

Quiet enough to learn from both success and failure.

Disciplined enough to keep justice tethered to humanity.

Repair, Responsibility, and the Lives We Are Living

Conflict does not only occur in public spaces. It takes shape within us, surfaces in our relationships, and often appears at the intersection of the work and the lives we are trying to live. For Black men in justice movements, this tension is constant. We are fighting for the conditions that allow people to live with dignity, safety, and freedom — while living those lives ourselves.

Repair is part of that complexity. When conflict causes harm — through missteps, miscommunication, or moments where power is mishandled — leadership requires accountability. Repair does not mean erasing mistakes or pretending harm didn't occur. It means acknowledging impact, taking responsibility, and committing to do better. When practiced with humility and care, repair strengthens movements rather than weakening them.

But repair also has to include ourselves.

Many leaders before us gave everything to the work, and home suffered. Relationships strained.

Families carried the cost. Others stepped away from the work entirely to protect their personal lives, sometimes disappearing from movements they helped build. Both paths reflect the weight of this tension.

I don't have a definitive answer for how to resolve it. I know this struggle personally — the travel, the meetings, the constant focus, the pull to be present everywhere except where you are. I've missed opportunities in movement spaces to be home. And I've seen how constant travel and visibility take a toll on family and relationships. Over time, I've learned this is not a problem to solve once, but a balance to revisit again and again.

The spotlight can be intoxicating. It can feel validating. It can also become addictive. Without grounding, it pulls us away from the very values we claim to be fighting for.

What has helped me is intentional reflection and accountability — regular check-ins with myself, honest conversations with people I respect and trust, confidants willing to tell me when I'm drifting. This kind of grounding doesn't eliminate the tension, but it keeps it visible.

Leadership with integrity requires us to remember that we are living the lives we say we want to protect. The work is about people — including ourselves and those closest to us. If the work demands that we abandon care, connection, and presence, then we have to ask hard questions about how we are doing it.

Again, this is not about perfection. It is about growth. We will misjudge moments. What matters is intentionality and self-accountability — the willingness to pause, to repair, and to realign with the north star.

That north star remains justice — not as an abstract ideal, but as collective liberation. Freedom that creates healthy, safe, and thriving communities rooted in love and respect.

Philip Agnew and the Reminder That Matters

As this chapter comes to a close, I'm reminded of leaders who have carried this ethic forward in real time — leaders who understood early that justice work is sustained not by spectacle, but by people.

Philip Agnew is one of those leaders. I first met Philip through Young People For, a program of People For the American Way, where I was working at the time. During those years, he was also one of the founders of the Dream Defenders. Even then, his leadership stood out. Not because he sought attention, but because he stayed focused on the work. He named injustice clearly, challenged systems directly, and remained accountable to the people most affected by the conditions he was organizing against.

What I admired then — and continue to admire now — is his clarity about what matters. Philip has consistently resisted the pull of spectacle and reminded movements to stay rooted in purpose.

> *"We have to remember that this work is about people, not moments."*
>
> — Philip Agnew

That reminder carries weight here. In a time when visibility can feel like validation and platforms can become distractions, Philip's words pull us back to the core of the work. They echo the lessons of those who came before us and reinforce the discipline required to lead with integrity in the present. For Black men navigating leadership in justice movements and adjacent spaces, that grounding is essential. It keeps us focused when conflict arises and steadies us when responsibility feels heavy. Justice work is not sustained by applause. It is sustained by care. Not by spotlight, but by commitment.

Staying Grounded While the Work Continues

Leadership in justice work does not offer clean endings. It offers responsibility that unfolds over time.

For Black men navigating power, conflict, and care, the work asks us to hold tension without being consumed by it. To repair harm without abandoning ourselves. To stay committed without losing sight of the lives we are living. This is not a balance we achieve once. It is a practice we return to over and over again.

We live the lives we say we are fighting for.

That truth complicates everything. It means the work does not stop at the meeting, the march, or the moment of visibility. It follows us home. It shows up in our relationships, our health, our presence, and our capacity to remain human in the midst of pressure. When the work pulls us away from care, connection, and grounding, it asks us to pause and reflect — not to retreat, but to realign.

There is no perfect formula for this. Some moments will require sacrifice. Others will require restraint. What matters is intention. The willingness to check ourselves. The courage to listen when something feels off. The discipline to stay accountable to the values we claim to hold.

This is where leadership becomes less about position and more about posture. The Bold Quiet Warrior does not hide when the work becomes difficult and does not disappear in the name of endurance. They remain grounded enough to repair harm, humble enough to learn, and disciplined enough to keep people at the center of the work.

Justice, in this sense, is not an abstract destination. It is a way of moving through the world. A commitment to collective liberation that creates space for people to live, grow, and thrive with dignity. Conflict will arise. Mistakes will be made. What sustains the work is thoughtfulness and care — for the mission, for the community, and for ourselves.

The work continues. And so must we.

The Interior Work

*"I learned that courage was not the absence of
fear, but the triumph over it."*

— Nelson Mandela

Nelson Mandela — a freedom fighter who spent 27
years imprisoned for resisting apartheid and later
became South Africa's first democratically elected
president — understood courage in a way few leaders
ever will.

Courage changes as we grow. When we are young
in the work, courage feels like stepping up to the
challenge right in front of us. With time, it becomes
something quieter — the steady choice to stay rooted
when fear, pressure, or expectation try to pull us off
center. Mandela's words remind us that fear is not the
enemy; losing ourselves to it is. For Black men, that
distinction matters. We have lived long enough with the
world projecting fear onto us that we learn early how to
carry our own without letting it define us.

By the time we reach positions of influence, the
conflict is no longer about whether we are brave. It is
about how we hold our courage without letting the
weight of responsibility harden us. It is about how we
stay open, disciplined, and whole in spaces that reward
performance but rarely honor truth. That tension — the

one between what the world demands and what our spirit requires — is where this chapter begins.

This is the interior work of leadership. The part no one sees. The part that determines whether we lead from reaction or from purpose. Institutions can stretch us thin. Movements can ask more than we have. Expectations — our own and others' — can press against the edges of our capacity. But the Bold Quiet Warrior knows that steadiness is not the absence of emotion; it is the practice of returning to ourselves again and again, even when the world pulls at us.

Earlier chapters traced how we learned responsibility, how we stepped into power, how we intervened when challenges demanded it. This chapter turns inward to ask a different question: What keeps us whole while we carry all of that? What disciplines, what grounding, what clarity allows us to move through fear without being shaped by it?

Because courage, for us, has never been loud. It has never been about proving anything to anyone. It has always been the quiet decision to move with intention — to stay aligned with who we are, to honor the people who shaped us, and to lead from a place that fear cannot touch.

What Grounds Us

The practices that sustain us grow with us. They reveal themselves as our leadership deepens. None of this is easy. I know firsthand how hard it can be to move through fear, to push forward when doubt whispers in your ear — not doubt about the work itself, but doubt about our own capacity to rise to it. That quiet uncertainty can follow us into rooms where we are expected to be steady, decisive, unshakable. It can shadow our steps even when our track record clearly says we belong.

For many of us, that doubt is not a flaw. It is a residue — of impostor syndrome, of survival strategies we learned early, of the ways we were taught to shrink ourselves just enough to stay safe. Those habits can become so familiar that we don't even recognize them as limits. They feel like discipline, like humility, like caution. But over time, they can keep us from stepping fully into the power we've earned.

The inner practices are how we break that pattern. They are how we return to ourselves. They are how we build the confidence that does not depend on applause or permission.

For me, that work begins in quiet. Meditation has become a way to settle the noise, to hear my own voice beneath the expectations of others. Exercise — especially riding my bike — gives me space to breathe, to clear my mind, to reconnect with the part of me that is steady even when the world feels unsteady. Those moments awaken the Bold Quiet Warrior within me. They remind me that courage is not a feeling; it is a practice.

We all have to find that place within ourselves — the space where fear loosens its grip and clarity can rise. For me it begins in quiet, in movement, in the simple act of returning to myself before the world gets loud again. That inner steadiness is not passive. It is a discipline built over time, returned to again and again, especially when leadership asks more than feels possible. The challenge is not knowing where the path ends. The challenge is trusting yourself enough to keep moving along it.

These practices are not accessories to leadership. They are the foundation. They are what allow us to carry weight without being crushed by it, to move with purpose even when the path is unclear, and to lead from a place that fear cannot touch.

Unlearning

Unlearning is its own kind of practice. It takes time, intention, and community. Many of the habits we carry into leadership were formed long before we ever stepped into positions of influence. Some were taught to us directly; others we picked up as protection. And even when those habits kept us safe, they can also keep us small. For Black men, unlearning is not about rejecting who we've been. It is about releasing what no longer serves the leader we are becoming.

I learned early what it meant to be held in community. I grew up surrounded by people who stayed connected to African culture, who understood the power of lineage, ritual, and collective care. That environment taught me to seek out my elders, to listen to their stories, to let their wisdom shape my own. It also taught me to seek out other Black men — brothers who were navigating their own journeys, carrying their own questions, building their own strength. That multigenerational approach has been one of the most important parts of my growth. It reminds me that leadership is not a solitary act. It is a shared practice.

Being in community with other Black men has helped me unlearn the instinct to shrink. In those spaces — formal and informal — I've facilitated conversations that surface trauma, fear, and the quiet burdens we rarely name. But those same conversations also reveal possibility. They lead to problem-solving, to clarity, to a deeper understanding of what we carry and what we can release. When we speak honestly with one another, we loosen the grip of impostor syndrome. We interrupt the stories that tell us we are not enough. We remember that we are not alone.

I've come to believe that positive thoughts lead to positive outcomes. How we see ourselves shapes how we move through the world. That belief is why I often return to an asset-framing mindset — a concept developed by Trabian Shorters, founder and CEO of the BMe Community and a leading voice in reshaping how Black people are described and valued in public life. Shorters created Asset-Framing® as a narrative practice that defines people by their aspirations and contributions before acknowledging their challenges. Asset framing is not about ignoring struggle. It is about naming our worth first — because the world needs to see Black men as assets worth investing in, and more importantly, we need to invest in ourselves with that same conviction.

Unlearning is not a one-time event. It is a continuous return to truth. It is the work of shedding what was necessary for survival but no longer necessary for leadership. It is the practice of choosing expansion over shrinking, clarity over fear, and community over isolation. And like all inner work, it grows stronger when we do it together.

Community as Orientation

Community has always been central to my leadership. It is why I do this work — and, in my view, why anyone should. Leadership disconnected from community loses its grounding. It becomes abstract. Community keeps us rooted in purpose and accountable to people, not just outcomes.

You cannot understand how to impact community if you are not connected to it. That connection has to be personal. It has to include spaces of support and spaces of learning. Community keeps us grounded and on task. It reminds us why the work matters and who it is for. In many ways, it is our superpower.

That superpower does not look the same for everyone — nor should it. Black men come from different backgrounds, regions, cultures, and traditions. That diversity is not a weakness. It is a strength that sharpens our leadership when we have the discipline to honor it.

That discipline matters because myths about Black manhood are persistent. They flatten us. They limit us. They tell us who we are supposed to be instead of allowing us to lead from who we actually are. Community helps us resist those myths. It reflects us back to ourselves with honesty and care. It reminds us that leadership is not about fitting a mold, but about showing up fully and staying accountable to one another.

This is why community must remain centered. Not as an afterthought. Not as a backdrop. But as the ground we stand on as we lead.

A Return to Practice

Courage, in the end, is not something we arrive at. It is something we return to. Again and again. Through practice. Through unlearning. Through community. Through the quiet work of believing in ourselves even when the path ahead is not fully visible.

Leadership does not require certainty. It requires commitment. The willingness to begin without knowing the end. The discipline to stay grounded when doubt whispers. The humility to remain connected to people who keep us honest and whole.

For Black men, that grounding has always been collective. We have never led alone — even when the world tried to convince us we had to.

This chapter is not a prescription. It is an invitation. To tend to the inner life with the same seriousness we bring to public responsibility. To invest in practices that sustain us. To unlearn what kept us safe but no longer serves us. And to remain rooted in community — not as a backdrop to leadership, but as its source.

The Bold Quiet Warrior does not rush toward certainty. He builds capacity. He stays grounded. And when the path is unclear, he moves — not because the fear is gone, but because the grounding is real.

Moral Responsibility When Power Is Real

The moral question at the heart of this chapter is simple, but not easy:

What does it mean for Black men to hold real power inside institutions that were never designed for justice — and how do we remain accountable to people when authority, access, and consequence are no longer theoretical?

This is the moment where leadership stops being aspirational and becomes consequential. Where values are no longer tested in rhetoric, but in decisions that shape lives, policies, and futures. For Black men, this moment carries particular weight. We are often invited into institutions as symbols of progress, while being constrained by structures that resist transformation. We are asked to lead change without disrupting comfort, to represent justice without unsettling power.

Holding that contradiction requires more than good intentions. It requires clarity about who we are accountable to — and what we are willing to risk.

"Justice is not about charity. It's about changing the structures that make charity necessary."

— Rev. Dr. William J. Barber II

Rev. Barber's words refuse distraction. They remind us that justice is not performative, not transactional, and not satisfied by access alone. They call us to examine whether our leadership challenges systems or merely manages their consequences.

Power changes the work. Not because justice suddenly becomes less urgent, but because authority introduces consequence. Decisions no longer live in theory. They shape budgets, policies, access, and outcomes. Institutions are designed to preserve themselves. They reward compliance, manage dissent, and often absorb critique without changing behavior. When Black men step into positions of influence inside these systems, we are asked to navigate a narrow path — to represent justice without unsettling power, to lead change without disrupting comfort, to be visible without being threatening.

That tension is not accidental. It is structural.

Holding power in these spaces requires more than good intentions. It requires clarity about who we are accountable to and what we are willing to risk. It demands discipline — not just in how we speak, but in how we decide, how we prioritize, and how we respond when pressure mounts.

For many Black men, this is where leadership becomes isolating. The expectations are high. The margins are thin. The consequences of missteps are amplified. And the temptation to compromise — to soften language, delay action, or accept incrementalism as inevitability — can feel like survival.

But moral responsibility does not disappear when power becomes real. It sharpens.

Justice, as Rev. Barber reminds us, is not about managing harm. It is about changing the conditions that produce it. That distinction matters deeply inside institutions. It forces us to ask whether our leadership is transforming systems or simply administering their outcomes more humanely.

This is not a call for recklessness. It is a call for intentional courage.

Bold enough to name injustice clearly, even when it disrupts comfort.

Quiet enough to listen for what the moment requires, not what the institution prefers.

Disciplined enough to remember that access is not the same as impact.

This chapter explores what it means to hold authority without losing integrity. To navigate institutional resistance without becoming cynical. And to remain accountable to people — not positions — when leadership carries real consequence.

Because when power is real, neutrality is not an option. And silence is never neutral.

When Power Had to Be Used

There are moments inside institutions when tension stops being background noise and becomes unavoidable.

One of those moments came when the founder of the organization — a white man with significant public visibility — used the N-word during a podcast conversation. He was speaking with a Black guest and appeared to believe that invoking the word would somehow neutralize its power. I don't believe there was malice in the intent. But intent was not the issue. It was not his word to use.

What followed was immediate and visceral. Black members of our programs — young people, organizers, ministers, elected officials — reached out in anger, confusion, and disappointment. Calls. Emails. Text messages. The people closest to the work felt betrayed, not only by what was said, but by what it revealed about who felt entitled to define the boundaries of racial discourse.

What unsettled me most was not the incident itself. It was how the organization responded — or failed to.

There was no urgency. No clear acknowledgment of harm. No immediate signal that leadership understood the gravity of what had happened. Silence filled the space where accountability should have been. And that silence landed hardest on Black staff, who were left to absorb the fallout without institutional backing.

I was a senior director at the time — close enough to power to feel its weight, but not seated at the highest decision-making table. I was often asked to speak publicly on racial justice issues on behalf of the organization. I carried the language outward. But internally, the structures had not yet caught up to the responsibility that language demanded.

When I learned of the incident, I was direct. I made clear that we needed to act — not defensively, not performatively, but with intention. There was real work ahead: listening to the people who were harmed, acknowledging the failure clearly and publicly, and committing to changes that would go beyond an apology. That meant revisiting how the organization's culture handled racial accountability, not just what it said about race in public.

What I learned from that moment stays with me. Power inside institutions is real. It protects some people and exposes others. When crisis hits, the people closest to the harm are often asked to carry the most weight while receiving the least support. That is a structural problem, and naming it out loud — even when it's uncomfortable — is part of what integrity requires.

Leadership in those moments is not about heroics. It is about accountability. It means staying grounded when the pressure is to move on. It means insisting that repair is real and not performative. And it means remembering that our presence in these institutions carries responsibility — not just for outcomes, but for culture.

Holding the Line Without Losing Yourself

There is a particular kind of pressure that comes with being one of the few Black men in a room where decisions are made. It is not always overt. Sometimes it is as subtle as a glance, a pivot in conversation, or the quiet expectation that you will translate the urgency of the work into something the institution can absorb without disruption.

I have felt that pressure. I've watched it shape the behavior of Black colleagues who came in with fire and left with caution — not because the fire went out, but because the institution kept teaching them that fire was the wrong tool.

Holding the line means refusing to let that happen without naming it. It means staying grounded in your values even when the institution offers comfort in exchange for compliance. It means speaking when the room goes quiet because no one else will, and listening when you need to hear what the people closest to the work actually need.

It also means knowing what you can and cannot change from where you stand, and being honest with yourself about the difference. Not every battle can be won from inside an institution. Some work requires building from outside. Some moments require you to stay and push. Discernment is the discipline that tells you which is which.

Holding the line is not the same as being inflexible. It is the practice of staying connected to your purpose even as the landscape shifts around you. It is the willingness to adapt tactics without abandoning values. And it is the commitment to remain accountable — to the people the work is meant to serve, to the colleagues who are watching, and to yourself.

Black men who lead with this kind of integrity do not always make the headlines. But their influence is real. It shapes culture. It builds trust. It creates the conditions where other people feel safe enough to bring their full selves into the work.

That is the kind of power worth holding.

The Weight of Representing

There is another dimension of power that Black men in institutional leadership carry, and it is rarely discussed with honesty: the weight of representation.

When you are one of few, every decision you make is read against the backdrop of what it means for people who look like you. A misstep is not just your misstep — it becomes evidence. A success is not just your success — it becomes a symbol. That pressure can quietly reshape how we move, what we say, and who we allow ourselves to be in professional spaces.

I've watched brothers carry this weight in silence — performing competence, managing perception, calculating how much of themselves to reveal. It is exhausting. And it is a form of labor that rarely gets named, let alone compensated.

Part of leading from wholeness in institutional spaces is learning to put that weight down without abandoning responsibility. It means refusing to let the anxiety of representation replace genuine accountability. It means understanding that your first obligation is not to manage how Black men are perceived, but to lead with integrity for the people the work is meant to serve.

That distinction is subtle but important. When we lead primarily from representation anxiety, we make decisions that protect image rather than impact. When we lead from integrity, we make decisions that honor people, even when they are costly.

Black men in positions of power do not have to carry the burden of proving our worthiness alone. We are worthy. The work is to lead from that truth, and to help build institutions where that truth does not have to be earned over and over again.

The Work of the Bold Quiet Warrior Under Pressure

Leadership under pressure reveals character. It strips away the language and exposes what we actually believe and what we are actually willing to do.

The Bold Quiet Warrior does not lead only when conditions are favorable. He leads when the conditions are difficult, when the stakes are high, when the comfortable path is clear and the right path is harder. He leads when staying silent would be easier, when going along would cost less, when pushing back might cost something real.

That kind of leadership is not dramatic. It is disciplined. It shows up in the decision to speak when silence is expected. In the willingness to stay engaged when disengagement would be safer. In the commitment to keep people at the center of the work, even when institutions try to pull focus toward systems, timelines, or optics.

Moral responsibility, when power is real, requires this discipline every day. Not as a performance, but as a practice. It requires leaders who know their values clearly enough to act from them even when the pressure is high.

This is hard work. It is also necessary work. And it is the work that moves justice forward, not just in moments of crisis, but in the accumulated decisions of daily leadership.

The work is no longer about proving we belong. It is about building something worthy of the trust we have been given. That is the moral responsibility of Black men when power is real. That is the work of the Bold Quiet Warrior.

PART IV

Staying Oriented in the Work

Justice work asks us to stay committed when the road is long, the progress is slow, and the reasons for leading are harder to see. This final section returns to the interior of leadership, asking what keeps Black men grounded, purposeful, and oriented toward justice when everything else is in motion.

Why You're Leading

"The question is not whether we have the ability to lead. The question is whether we have the commitment to lead with integrity."

— Diallo K. Brooks

There are moments in the work when the clarity that brought you here begins to blur.

The meetings multiply. The demands increase. The urgency never lets up. And somewhere in the middle of all of it, a question surfaces that can feel dangerous to ask: Why am I still doing this?

It is not a question of weakness. It is a question of honesty. And it is one of the most important questions a leader can sit with.

For Black men in justice work, the answer to that question is not always simple. Some of us came to this work through personal experience — shaped by what we witnessed in our families, our neighborhoods, our communities. Some came through conviction — a belief that the world should be more just and a sense of responsibility to help make it so. Some came through relationships — following the example of people we admired, stepping into spaces where we were needed.

However we arrived, the why that brought us here is what sustains us when the work gets hard. It is the thread we have to keep returning to, especially when everything around us is asking us to react, to perform, to prove, or to give up.

This chapter is about that thread. It is about the importance of knowing why you lead — not the polished version you share in speeches, but the real version that lives underneath. The one shaped by your story, your values, and your understanding of what this work is actually for.

When Why Gets Blurry

Leadership without a clear why is leadership without roots. It can still move forward, but it moves reactively — chasing momentum, managing optics, responding to whatever is most urgent. Without roots, it cannot sustain itself. And without roots, it cannot grow.

I have seen this pattern in myself and in others. It usually starts quietly. The work that once felt meaningful begins to feel mechanical. Decisions that once came from clarity start coming from habit or obligation. The people who used to feel central begin to feel like variables in a problem that won't resolve.

When that happens, the why has gone underground. It hasn't disappeared — but it needs to be excavated again. It needs to be brought back into the light and examined with honesty.

Sometimes the excavation reveals that the original why still holds. That the fire is still there, just covered by exhaustion or frustration or the accumulated weight of doing the work in conditions that are never quite right.

In those cases, the practice is about rest, reconnection, and renewed commitment.

Other times, the excavation reveals something harder to sit with: that the why has changed. That the work we're doing no longer aligns with the purpose that called us forward. That it may be time to step back, redirect, or reimagine how we contribute.

Both of these are legitimate discoveries. Neither of them means failure. They are signs that leadership is a living practice, not a fixed destination. They are invitations to stay honest with ourselves even when honesty is uncomfortable.

Beyond Blind Following

One of the quiet dangers in justice work is the temptation to lead by following — to orient ourselves entirely around what movements, institutions, or respected figures tell us matters, without examining whether that aligns with what we actually believe.

This is different from learning from others. Learning is essential. But there is a difference between learning from others and outsourcing your own sense of direction to them. One deepens the work; the other hollows it out.

Black men have often been expected to follow without question — to defer, to comply, to stay in our lane. That expectation has come from outside our communities and, painfully, from within them as well. It has been dressed up as loyalty, as unity, as the price of belonging.

Leadership requires us to push back on that expectation, not to be contrary, but to be honest. Movements need people who think critically, who ask hard questions, who are willing to name when the emperor has no clothes even when everyone else in the room is clapping. That kind of honest engagement is not disloyalty. It is the most important thing a committed leader can offer.

Staying connected to your own why is how you do that. It is how you remain grounded in your purpose even when the surrounding culture is pulling you in a different direction. It is how you stay accountable not just to the movement, but to the people the movement is meant to serve.

The Why Beneath the Why

I have asked myself this question more times than I can count: What is the real reason I'm doing this?

Not the version I've been trained to articulate. Not the language I reach for in meetings or presentations. But the truth underneath — the one that lives in my body, that shows up when I'm tired and honest and the performance has dropped away.

For me, the answer has always come back to people. To the faces of young Black men I've met across this country who carry brilliance and purpose and possibility, and who are navigating systems that were never designed to see them clearly. To the communities I come from and the people who shaped me. To the leaders who went before us and gave everything they had, not for recognition, but because they believed the future was worth it.

That is what the work is for. Not the campaign. Not the report. Not the platform. The people.

When I lose sight of that, I know I've drifted. And when I return to it, the work finds its weight again — its meaning, its direction, its reason for continuing even when the conditions are hard.

Your why might look different from mine. It should. Leadership is not one-size-fits-all, and purpose is not transferable. But every Black man who leads with integrity has a why that is real and specific and deeply personal. The work is to find it, to name it, and to return to it often.

Keeping the Purpose Alive

The purpose that calls us forward cannot be maintained by willpower alone. It has to be tended.

Tending looks different for different people. For some, it means regular time in reflection — prayer, journaling, meditation, or simply sitting with the questions that matter most. For others, it means returning to the communities that grounded you, hearing directly from the people the work is meant to serve, being reminded in the most concrete possible way why any of this matters.

For many of us, it means staying in honest conversation with other leaders who are navigating the same terrain. Not to compare notes on strategy, but to be real with one another about the doubt, the fatigue, and the moments when the why gets hard to see. That kind of honesty among leaders is rare and valuable. It keeps us from performing certainty we don't feel and pretending steadiness that hasn't been earned.

Community, as always, is part of how purpose stays alive. The work is collective. The meaning is collective. And the renewal that comes from being in right relationship with people who share your values and challenge your growth is not a luxury. It is a necessity.

Know why you're leading. Return to it often. Let it shape how you show up, what you prioritize, and what you're willing to risk. That purpose — specific, honest, and yours — is what allows leadership to endure. It is what keeps the work from becoming just work. And it is what connects you, across time, to every leader who came before you and carried the same commitment forward.

Lead from your why. It will not always be loud. But it will always be real.

Leading in the Moment

*"You don't make progress by standing on the
sidelines, whimpering and complaining. You
make progress by implementing ideas."*

— Shirley Chisholm

Shirley Chisholm never waited for perfect conditions. She moved. She pushed. She led in real time, with what she had, guided by a clarity about what mattered and a refusal to let the moment pass without acting on it.

That is what this chapter is about.

There comes a point where preparation must give way to action. Where the why you have been refining, the values you have been deepening, and the community you have been building all get tested in the actual moment of leadership. Not the rehearsed version. The real one. The one where the stakes are high, the conditions are imperfect, and the decision cannot wait.

Leading in the moment is not about spontaneity. It is about readiness. It is what happens when preparation meets reality, when grounding meets pressure, and when the person you have been building yourself to be is asked to show up right now.

The Defend the Black Vote Campaign

One of the clearest examples of leading in the moment from my own experience came during the 2020 election cycle through the Defend the Black Vote campaign.

The political landscape that year was unlike anything I had navigated before. Disinformation was everywhere. Voter suppression efforts were intensifying. And Black voters — particularly in Southern states — were being targeted with a precision that was both sophisticated and deeply familiar. The tactics had changed. The intent had not.

We did not have unlimited resources. We did not have a perfect playbook. What we had was clarity about what was at stake, trust in the communities we were working with, and a commitment to respond to what was actually happening on the ground rather than what looked good on paper.

That meant making decisions quickly. It meant pivoting when the message was not landing. It meant listening to community members who understood their terrain better than any outside strategist could. It meant trusting the leadership of people closest to the work, even when that meant stepping back and supporting rather than directing.

There were moments during that campaign when I had to act on incomplete information. When the right answer wasn't clear and the cost of waiting was too high. When the only path forward was to move with what I had, stay accountable to the people I was serving, and adjust as the situation became clearer.

That is leading in the moment. Not heroics. Not certainty. Just the disciplined, grounded practice of showing up where you are, with what you have, guided by your values and your commitment to the people who are counting on you.

When the Moment Asks More Than You Planned For

Not every critical moment comes with advance notice. Some of the most important leadership decisions I have made came in spaces I didn't fully control, on timelines I didn't set, in response to circumstances I didn't anticipate.

That is the nature of real leadership. It doesn't ask permission. It doesn't wait for the ideal moment. It surfaces in the middle of everything else and asks: What are you going to do right now?

I have learned that the answer to that question is shaped almost entirely by what you have built before the moment arrives. Not your résumé or your platform, but your character. Your grounding. Your clarity about what you value and who you are accountable to. Your capacity to stay present when the pressure is high and the path is not obvious.

This is why the interior work matters so much. It is why community matters. It is why knowing your why is not just a reflective exercise but a practical foundation. When the moment arrives, you do not have time to locate your values from scratch. They have to already be there, built into how you see and respond to the world.

Black men in justice work often lead in moments that others have walked away from. We show up in communities that have been abandoned, in institutions that have been ignored, in conversations that no one else wanted to have. That kind of leadership is not glamorous. But it is consequential. And it requires exactly the kind of grounded, prepared readiness that this book has been building toward.

Staying Accountable in Real Time

Leading in the moment also means staying accountable when the moment is over.

Real-time leadership is not just about the decision itself. It is about how you show up afterward. Did you stay true to your values? Did you keep people at the center? Did you make space for others to lead alongside you, or did the pressure push you into patterns you have been trying to move away from?

Accountability in real time does not mean constant self-criticism. It means honest reflection. It means being willing to ask hard questions and receive honest answers. It means repairing quickly when something went wrong and learning clearly when something went right.

The leaders I have respected most in my life are not the ones who never made mistakes in the moment. They are the ones who stayed accountable afterward. Who acknowledged what happened, took responsibility for their part, and kept moving with integrity. That consistency — between how they led in the moment and how they held themselves after — is what made their leadership trustworthy over time.

That is what real-time leadership asks of us. Not perfection. Presence. Accountability. And the willingness to stay in the work even when the moment has cost us something.

The Practice of Leading Now

Everything in this book has been pointing here.

To the moment in front of you. To the community that needs your leadership. To the work that is waiting not for the right conditions, but for the committed leader who is willing to show up as they are and do what needs to be done.

Leading in the moment is the fullest expression of everything we have been building — the grounding, the wholeness, the purpose, the accountability, the community. It is where all of that preparation becomes real, in the actual choices we make, the way we show up, and the impact we have on the people around us.

Leadership does not wait for ideal conditions. It asks you to show up where you are, with what you have, guided by your values and your vision, and to lead — right here, in this moment.

Holding the North Star

There is a particular kind of disorientation that comes from doing justice work over a long period of time.

It is not the disorientation of not knowing what to do. Most of us know, at some level, what needs to happen. The disorientation is subtler than that. It comes from the gap between what we know and what we can seem to make real. From the distance between the world we are trying to build and the one we are actually navigating. From the accumulated weight of working hard and watching progress move slowly, or not at all, or backward.

That kind of disorientation can quietly reshape us. Not all at once, but gradually — the way water wears stone. Over time, the urgency softens into fatigue. The vision narrows into tactical thinking. The commitment to people gets crowded out by the demands of process, politics, and institutional survival. And somewhere in the distance, the north star that once oriented us begins to feel less like a guide and more like a memory.

This chapter is about not letting that happen.

What the North Star Actually Is

When I use the phrase north star, I am not talking about an abstract ideal or an inspirational slogan. I am talking about the specific, concrete vision of justice that called you into this work and that continues to give it meaning.

For every leader, that north star has a shape. It is rooted in experience — in what you have seen, what you have lost, what you have been part of building. It is shaped by the people who matter most to you and the communities you are most accountable to. It is not transferable, and it is not generic.

The north star might be a world where Black boys and girls grow up with the full expectation of safety, dignity, and opportunity. It might be the transformation of systems that have caused generational harm. It might be the vision of a community where leadership is shared, care is abundant, and people are free to contribute fully. It might be something even more specific — a school, a neighborhood, a generation, a relationship between power and people that has never fully existed but that you can imagine clearly enough to work toward.

Whatever it is, it belongs to you. And holding it means returning to it regularly — not only when the work is going well, but especially when it is not.

The Gap Between Vision and Reality

I have spent most of my career working at the intersection of vision and reality. I have been in spaces where the vision was clear, the strategy was strong, and the people were ready, and the work still moved slowly. I have seen campaigns built with extraordinary care produce results that fell short of what was needed. I have watched institutions commit to justice in language and resist it in practice.

That gap — between what is and what should be — is where justice work actually lives. And navigating it without losing your direction requires something that data and strategy alone cannot provide. It requires orientation. It requires the ability to look at conditions that are genuinely discouraging and still know which way you are pointed.

The north star does that. It doesn't deny the difficulty. It doesn't promise quick resolution. But it holds the direction. And holding the direction is what allows us to keep moving when the terrain is hard and the finish line is not yet visible.

Researchers who study community change and organizational effectiveness often find that the leaders who sustain their work over time are not the ones who are most talented or most resourced. They are the ones who remain most clearly oriented to purpose. They make decisions differently. They build relationships differently. They stay engaged through adversity differently. Not because they are immune to discouragement, but because they know what they are working toward and why.

That orientation is not passive. It is not just a feeling of inspiration that sustains you on hard days. It is an active discipline. It shows up in how you frame problems, how you communicate with your team, how you decide what to prioritize and what to let go. It shapes the culture around you, because people can feel when a leader is oriented toward something real.

When the North Star Gets Hard to See

There will be seasons when the north star is hard to locate.

I have been in those seasons. Times when the setbacks were significant enough to make the vision feel naive. Times when I wondered whether the work was making enough of a difference to justify what it was costing. Times when the gap between vision and reality felt not like a challenge to navigate but like a wall to stare at.

What I've learned in those seasons is that the north star doesn't move — but we do. We drift, sometimes without realizing it. We get pulled by urgency, by conflict, by the thousand small decisions that accumulate into patterns. And eventually we look up and realize that what we're pointing toward is no longer what we intended.

The practice of holding the north star is, in part, the practice of noticing when we've drifted and choosing to realign. Not with judgment, but with honesty. Not with self-criticism, but with the simple recognition that we have moved and need to find our way back.

Community is essential to this practice. Some of the most important moments of realignment in my own leadership have come through conversation — with peers who named something I had stopped seeing, with mentors who asked questions that opened things up, with younger leaders whose clarity reminded me of what I had originally come to do. We need people around us who know our north star and who will tell us the truth when we have lost sight of it.

Carrying the North Star Forward

What endures across all of these chapters is not a set of instructions but a set of commitments.

A commitment to staying grounded in values — not just naming them, but returning to them when the pressure is high and the easier path is clear.

A commitment to keeping people at the center — not as abstract beneficiaries, but as the living, specific human beings whose dignity and freedom are what the work is actually for.

A commitment to aligning strategy with vision — not letting the urgency of the moment crowd out the clarity of the long game.

A commitment to balancing structure with humanity — building institutions that work without losing the warmth and care that make them worth building.

A commitment to leading with presence — not managing from a distance, but showing up fully, in real time, in the places where the work is actually happening.

A commitment to staying connected to community — not as an audience or a constituency, but as the ground beneath everything else.

A commitment to growth — remaining open to what the work is teaching, willing to unlearn what no longer serves, and honest enough to keep becoming.

And a commitment to returning to the north star — again and again and again. Not as a performance of purpose, but as an act of fidelity. To the vision. To the people. To the work that matters most.

The north star does not move. But we do. And leadership, at its best, is the practice of finding our way back to it.

Closing: Staying in the Work

*"I can accept failure. Everyone fails at something.
But I can't accept not trying."*

— Michael Jordan

There is a kind of leadership that announces itself loudly — that names what it is, claims its place, and makes sure everyone in the room knows it has arrived. And then there is the kind that shows up quietly, does what needs to be done, and leaves the space better than it found it.

This book has been about the second kind.

Not because visibility is wrong. Not because Black men should diminish themselves or stay quiet when the moment calls for a clear voice. But because the kind of leadership that endures — the kind that holds communities together, sustains movements, and shapes the future — is most often the kind that is rooted, consistent, and grounded in something deeper than recognition.

We have moved through a lot of ground in these pages. We have talked about where leadership comes from and what pulls us away from it. We have explored what it means to lead from wholeness rather than depletion, to build for the long haul rather than the moment, to prepare the people who will carry the work forward when we step back. We have sat with the complexity of power, the necessity of inner practice, the weight of moral responsibility, and the discipline of staying oriented when the work is slow or the direction is unclear.

None of that is finished. None of it is ever fully resolved. Leadership is not a destination. It is a practice. And the practice continues.

What Staying Means

Staying in the work does not mean never stepping away. It does not mean burning yourself out in service of a cause that cannot sustain itself on your sacrifice. It does not mean staying in roles that have stopped serving the mission or relationships that have become harmful.

Staying means maintaining your commitment to justice even when the immediate context shifts. It means keeping the work alive inside you — the curiosity, the care, the conviction — even during the seasons when the external work is quiet. It means not letting cynicism settle in where hope once lived.

I have watched leaders leave the work. Sometimes it was necessary. Sometimes it was right. Sometimes it was a loss that a movement or institution never fully recovered from. And in many of those cases, what preceded the leaving was not a single dramatic moment but a slow erosion — of connection, of purpose, of the belief that the work was worth it.

Staying requires intention. It requires the practices and relationships and grounding that keep purpose alive even when conditions are discouraging. It requires knowing your why clearly enough to return to it when everything around you is pulling toward exit.

And it requires honesty. Honesty about what you can sustain and what you can't. About when rest is renewal and when distance is drift. About what the work needs from you right now and what it might need from you in a different form in the future.

What Chadwick Boseman Taught Us

I think often about Chadwick Boseman.

Not only because of what he created, but because of how he carried himself while creating it. Here was a man who knew, for a significant portion of his most visible years of work, that he was fighting a serious illness. And he showed up anyway. Not to prove something. Not to be celebrated. But because the work mattered and the people who would receive it mattered, and he was committed to giving them what he had while he still had it.

I do not share this to romanticize suffering or to hold self-sacrifice up as the model of leadership. I share it because Boseman's example points to something essential: staying in the work, at its deepest, is an act of love. It is the decision, made again and again in ordinary moments and extraordinary ones, to remain committed to something larger than yourself.

> *"Sometimes you need to feel the pain and sting of defeat to activate the real passion and purpose that God predestined inside of you."*
>
> — Chadwick Boseman

That purpose, once found and held with care, becomes the ground beneath us. And from that ground, we lead.

An African Proverb and a Final Word

There is a proverb that has stayed with me throughout the writing of this book:

"When the music changes, so does the dance."

Justice work is always changing. The conditions shift. The strategies evolve. The faces in the room change. What remains constant is the north star — the commitment to a more just world — and the people who are willing to keep showing up for it.

Black men have always been among those people. Not because the world made it easy, but because the commitment ran deeper than the obstacles. Not because we were asked, but because we understood, in ways that live below language, that this work belongs to us and we belong to it.

This book has been an invitation to go deeper into that belonging. To lead not from performance, but from purpose. Not from fear, but from groundedness. Not from isolation, but from community. To stay in the work with honesty and care. To build something worthy of the people who will inherit it.

The music will keep changing. Stay in the dance.

Lead right. Learn always.

About the Author

Diallo K. Brooks is a transformational executive, movement strategist, and civic leader with more than 25 years of national leadership in racial justice, public policy, civic engagement, and philanthropy.

He is the founder and Principal Strategist of Civic Vision Strategies, a Washington, DC-based consulting firm that works with organizations, coalitions, and institutions committed to building equity and power in underserved communities. His work bridges strategy and implementation, helping clients navigate complex political and social landscapes with clarity and purpose.

Diallo's career has taken him to the front lines of some of the most significant civic and justice campaigns in recent American history. He served as a strategist on the Defend the Black Vote campaign during the 2020 election cycle, a national effort to counter disinformation and voter suppression targeting Black communities. He co-chaired Black Youth Vote alongside Melanie Campbell and the National Coalition on Black Civic Participation, helping shape the infrastructure of Black youth civic engagement at a national level. Early in his career, he worked at the Rainbow PUSH Coalition under the late Rev. Jesse Jackson Sr., an experience that deepened his understanding of movement leadership and coalition building. He also served at the U.S. Department of Education, where his work focused on educational equity and access.

Across these roles, Diallo has been guided by a consistent conviction: that leadership, when practiced with integrity, care, and community, is the most powerful force available to us in the pursuit of justice.

He is also the author of the first volume of the Bold Quiet Warrior series, which explores the inner discipline of leadership and the practices that allow Black men to lead with wholeness and purpose. The series grows out of his deep belief that justice work needs Black men — not as symbols or emergency responders, but as rooted, committed participants in the life of our communities.

Diallo is a sought-after speaker, facilitator, and trainer who has worked with elected officials, grassroots organizers, nonprofit leaders, and emerging changemakers across the country. He believes that leadership development and movement building are inseparable, and that the most durable change happens when people are invested in and prepared to lead with purpose over the long haul.

He lives in the Washington, DC area.

Learn more at:
www.boldquietwarrior.com
www.civicvisionstrategies.com

A Tool for the Work

Leadership Commitments for Black Men in Justice Work

This appendix is offered as a practical resource — for personal reflection, team conversations, and facilitated discussions. Each commitment names a practice at the heart of this book. The questions are invitations, not evaluations. Sit with them honestly, and return to them often.

1. Stay Grounded in Values

Why this matters: Clarity about what we value is what allows us to lead with consistency, especially when pressure mounts and the easier path is clear. Values are not just what we believe — they are how we move.

A question to sit with: What are the two or three values that most consistently shape how you make decisions? When was the last time you were tested on them?

2. Keep People at the Center

Why this matters: Justice work is about people. Not systems, not metrics, not platforms — but the living, specific human beings whose dignity and freedom are what the work is actually for. When we lose sight of people, we lose our direction.

A question to sit with: In your current work, who are the specific people you are most accountable to? How often do you hear directly from them?

3. Align Strategy with Vision

Why this matters: Strategy without vision becomes reactive. Vision without strategy becomes abstract. The work that lasts is built at the intersection — where a clear picture of what we are working toward shapes how we act in the present.

A question to sit with: Does your current strategy reflect your long-term vision for justice? Where are the gaps?

4. Balance Structure with Humanity

Why this matters: Strong institutions need structure. But structure without care produces systems that serve themselves rather than the people they were built for. The goal is organizations and movements that are both effective and humane.

A question to sit with: In the spaces you lead or participate in, does structure support people or constrain them? What would it take to shift the balance?

5. Lead with Presence

Why this matters: Leadership that is distracted, performative, or absent cannot sustain trust. Presence — showing up fully, in real time, in the places where the work is happening — is one of the most powerful things a leader can offer.

A question to sit with: Where in your leadership do you tend to show up fully? Where do you tend to hold back or disengage? What shapes that difference?

6. Stay Connected to Community

Why this matters: Community is not the audience for leadership. It is the ground beneath it. When leaders lose connection to community, they lose the orientation that makes the work meaningful and the accountability that keeps it honest.

A question to sit with: How do you stay connected to the communities your work is meant to serve? What would it look like to deepen that connection?

7. Commit to Growth

Why this matters: Leadership is a practice, not a destination. The leaders who sustain impact over time are those who remain open to learning — willing to unlearn what no longer serves, honest about their limitations, and genuinely committed to becoming.

A question to sit with: What are you currently unlearning? What would you like to grow into as a leader in the next year?

8. Return to the North Star

Why this matters: The north star is the specific, concrete vision of justice that called you into this work and gives it meaning. We drift from it — through urgency, through fatigue, through the thousand small pulls of daily leadership. The practice is noticing when we've drifted and choosing to come back.

A question to sit with: What is your north star? When did you last return to it? Who in your life helps you stay oriented to it?

These commitments are the foundation of the Bold Quiet Warrior leadership framework. They are offered not as a checklist, but as a compass — something to return to as the work evolves and the conditions change.

For facilitation guides, speaking engagements, and leadership development resources, visit:
www.boldquietwarrior.com
www.civicvisionstrategies.com